Richard St. Barbe Baker

Baker

Child of the Trees

Richard St. Barbe Baker
Baker
Child of the Trees

by Paul Hanley

illustrated by Elizabeth Konn

BELLWOOD
PRESS

WILMETTE, ILLINOIS

Bellwood Press, Wilmette, Illinois
401 Greenleaf Avenue, Wilmette, Illinois 60091

23   22   21   20   4   3   2   1

Library of Congress Cataloging in Publication Data
Names: Hanley, Paul, author.
Title: Richard St. Barbe Baker : child of the trees / by Paul Hanley.
Other titles: Man of the trees.
Description: Wilmette, Illinois : Bellwood Press, [2020] | Series:
    Change maker ; volume 3 | Includes bibliographical references. |
    Audience: Ages 10–12 | Audience: Grades 4–6
Identifiers: LCCN 2020011316 (print) | LCCN 2020011317 (ebook)
    | ISBN 9781618511638 (paperback) | ISBN 9781618511652
    (kindle edition)
Subjects: LCSH: Baker, Richard St. Barbe, 1889–1982—Juvenile
    literature. |
    Conservationists—Biography—Juvenile literature. | Forest
    Conservation—History—Juvenile literature. | Chipko
    Movement—History—Juvenile literature.
Classification: LCC SD411.52.B39 H36 2020 (print) | LCC
    SD411.52.B39 (ebook) | DDC 333.72092 [B]—dc23
LC record available at https://lccn.loc.gov/2020011316
LC ebook record available at https://lccn.loc.gov/2020011317

Book and cover design by Patrick Falso
Illustrations by Elizabeth Konn

*For my grandchildren, Emma, Sabri, and Ingrid,
with the hope that their grandchildren will be able to enjoy
the world's forests.*

Contents

Acknowledgments

This is my second book on Richard St. Barbe Baker, the first being a full biography. To research that book, I received an Explorations Grant from the Canada Council for the Arts. Indirectly, then, the Council helped to make this version of the story possible.

Richard's literary trustee, Hugh Locke, granted permission to quote from his books, all now out of print.

I am particularly indebted to the University of Saskatchewan Library, University

Archives & Special Collections, Richard St. Barbe Baker fonds, and its staff for providing me the opportunity to sift through their extensive collection of Richard's papers, which yielded most of my material.

I would like to thanks several friends and fellow admirers of the Man of the Trees for their support: Robert White, David van Vliet, Hugh Locke, and Paul Mantle. My wife, Haleh Samimi, also helped me in many ways.

Introduction

"Our house is on fire! . . . I want you to panic!"[1]

Swedish youth Greta Thunberg's bold challenge to a conference of international leaders moved the world. After her brave speech to the World Economic Forum in 2019, Greta became known around the world. Today, she is the face of a growing movement of young people who feel the future of their planet is being threatened by climate change.

All over the world, young people are becoming aware that the environment is endangered. They are speaking up and joining a worldwide discussion about the actions humanity needs to take to protect its future. And many young people are going beyond words. They are taking personal action to protect the planet.

Could you help move the world like Greta Thunberg? Or like Felix Finkbeiner?

Felix Finkbeiner is another young environmentalist who is moving the world. When he was nine years old, his teacher asked him to write a short essay about the environment. Felix read about two people who helped protect the planet by planting millions of trees. One of these was Wangari Maathai, a Kenyan who organized women in her country to plant trees and restore their farmland. The other person was Richard St. Barbe Baker, whose fascinating story is told in this book.

Inspired by these environmental pioneers, Felix decided to start a children's movement to plant trees. The results were amazing. Today, the group he started, Plant-for-the-Planet, leads a United Nations' tree planting program. The organization has seventy-five thousand climate justice ambassadors, ages 8–14. Their goal is to help millions of people plant a trillion trees! Fourteen billion trees have been planted already.

You see—youth *can* move the world!

You have probably heard of Sir Isaac Newton. He is the famous scientist who discovered the laws of gravity. He once wrote that if he had "seen further" and made great scientific breakthroughs, it was because he had been "standing upon the shoulders of giants."[2] He meant that other scientists who lived before him had made discoveries that he built on to make even bigger discoveries about the way the world works.

Young activists like Greta and Felix are "standing on the shoulders" of environmental giants who went before them. One of these giants was Richard St. Barbe Baker, who spent his long life—ninety-two years—telling everyone he could, including tens of thousands of children, about the importance of trees and forests. He believed that planting trees could help prevent climate change. His most ambitious goal was to unite the whole world to work together to turn the Sahara, the world's largest desert, into a forest.

Richard's ideas about the need to protect the global environment were not well understood when he was alive. Although most people didn't appreciate how important they were, he never gave up trying to educate people about the importance of preserving and protecting the environment.

Today, scientists say we need to plant billons of trees to help cool our overheated climate. Today, just as Richard had proposed, twenty-one African countries are working together to plant a Great Green Wall of trees to help reforest the Sahara.[3]

In just one day, in August of 2019, millions of Ethiopians planted 350 million trees in twelve hours![4] They proved that people could accomplish amazing things very quickly when they work together, just as Richard St. Barbe Baker had said.

We can learn a lot from reading about the life of Richard St. Barbe Baker, known around the world as the Man of the Trees.[5] Perhaps you can learn how to plant trees and help to heal our planet, too.

1 / Child of the Trees

It was 1894. Five-year-old Richard Baker was lost in the forest. He had been warned not to wander off alone, but the big trees surrounding his home were calling him.

Since he was a toddler, he had helped his father plant thousands of trees. Other children played with toy soldiers. Richard marched about the seedbeds, saluting his new trees and popping off their seed caps with his toy sword. He moistened the soil with a little watering can and made hundreds of trips from the rain barrel to the seedlings.

Near the house, there was a sand pit to play in. He turned this little "desert" into a forest with the leafy twigs dropped by squirrels or the wind. These he placed in avenues leading to a castle, complete with a moat and drawbridge.

Richard had wandered deep into the dark forest. He was lost, but it didn't feel that way to him. He walked dreamily, losing all sense of time. High above, through the green canopy of leaves, light entered the forest in shafts, shining in the morning mists. He walked deeper into the forest, unafraid. Richard felt as if he had entered a temple of the woods. He sank to the ground in a state of great happiness, a state called *ecstasy*. All his senses and feelings came alive. He was alone but felt the trees and all the living creatures he loved were embracing him.

Sometimes people have a very strong feeling of joy and a sense that they are part of everything. This sense of being one with the world around us is called a *mystical* experience. Richard's mystical experience among the trees that day influenced the rest of his life.

After a long while, he awakened from his trance and found a path in the forest that led him home. When his parents scolded him for wandering off into the forest, he hardly noticed. He was more in love with trees than ever.

Richard was the eldest of five children. He learned to be a responsible son at an early age and was soon helping his parents take care of the family's land, which was located in Hampshire, in England.

His father was a kind man. Although he was a devout Christian, he welcomed people of all faiths and backgrounds to his house. The house was always open to everyone, and the family welcomed many visitors, who were often hoping for something to eat. They would often arrive first thing in the morning and would be greeted warmly by Richard's mother, who would invite them inside for a cup of tea.

Richard enjoyed school. He especially liked boxing, playing soccer, and learning about carpentry. During the holidays, he would work on the family's tree nursery.

His father was raising thousands of forest and ornamental trees from seeds. Richard helped with bed preparation, seeding, weeding, and transplanting until the trees were ready for sale. As soon as he could drive, he was trusted with delivering loads of trees to be newly planted in the neighborhood.

Richard's father also taught him how to manage forests. He learned how to measure trees to be used for lumber and which wood was the best for different purposes, such as building a table or a doorframe.

Richard was also a beekeeper. He built his own beehives out of old boxes, and soon he had sixteen hives, each producing up to two hundred and forty pounds of honey per year. Another of his interests was looking after horses. He became an expert rider and also learned how to gentle horses that had never been ridden.

Some members of the Baker family were great adventurers. One of his uncles was the explorer Samuel Baker, who once led a famous expedition to the source of the Nile River in Africa.

When Richard was a teenager, he began to hear stories of another uncle who was also named Richard. This uncle had gone to Canada as a pioneer and had written home about his new life. Richard loved the exciting bits, such as stories about fighting bears!

It took a few years to get his parents' blessing, but in 1909, twenty-year-old Richard sold his beehives. He used the money to buy a ticket to travel to Canada by ship. He then took a train to Saskatoon, Saskatchewan. By the time he reached his destination, he was 4100 miles from his home. He planned to become a pioneer farmer like his uncle.

2 / Pioneer, Student, Soldier

In the early 1900s, people could get land in Western Canada almost for free if they agreed to turn their land into a productive farm. Richard got a small farm at Beaver Creek near Saskatoon (now a city of 275,000). He also enrolled in Saskatoon's brand-new university.

Richard Baker was one of the first students at the University of Saskatchewan. With some friends, he built a shack—one of the first student residences—on campus. He was studying to be a Christian minister, and he often traveled on horseback to visit rural churches on Sundays. This part of Canada gets very cold in winter, and the temperature can drop as low as -49F. His winter journeys were bone-chilling.

To make a living, Richard wrote sports stories for the local newspaper and also worked as a ranch hand. It was through training and trading horses that he met Charlie Eagle, who was a member of the Dakota First Nation and lived on the Moosewoods Indian Reservation near Beaver Creek.

The Dakotas are one of the Indigenous peoples of Canada. While talking with Charlie and his family around their campfires, Richard learned about the way of life, values, and beliefs of the Dakota people. Later, Richard would say his conversations with Charlie opened up a new way of looking at nature and helped shape his views about protecting the environment.

Another thing that would shape his thinking was working as a lumberjack in Canada's northern forests.

At that time, the sawmill at Big River, Saskatchewan was among the largest in the world. Richard could see that, in the area around the sawmill, forests were being mistreated. Many trees were being cut down, and replanting was neglected. Because he loved trees so much, he was horrified. He could see that this kind of exploitation would eventually ruin the forests.

Richard decided to give up his dream of farming and return to England. He would become a forester, and he would learn even more about how to manage and protect trees.

Richard had been away four years, and he returned just in time for Christmas. His family was very happy to see him. Although he had originally hoped to enroll immediately in forestry school, his plans were delayed when the First World War broke out. On one hand, as a Christian, Richard did not want to participate in a war. On the other hand, he felt that in this case, it was his duty to join the army to protect his country.

During the war, Richard was put in charge of gathering and training thousands of horses for the army. He was very skilled at this job, which resulted in a promotion to the rank of captain.

He also went into battle and was wounded on three occasions. The first time, he was buried underneath rubble when his troop was hit with artillery fire.

When he was rescued, he was so badly injured that the medics thought he was dead. He was being sent home to be buried when someone noticed he was still bleeding—a sign of life. Instead of being sent to the graveyard, he went to the hospital.

Richard had a *near death experience* (or NDE) that day. During an NDE, a person's vital signs will drop, and he will appear to die briefly before being revived. Often he will have strange and wonderful experiences during the few minutes he is "dead." He might feel as if he is suspended in the air looking down at his own body. Sometimes people who experience NDEs report meeting spirits who comfort them, and this is what had happened to Richard. In his case, a vision of one of his fellow-soldiers who had been killed in battle came to console him. It was the first of five NDEs Richard would experience in his lifetime!

Once he recovered from his injury, Richard returned to service, but he was wounded again. This time, a horse fell on him, and broke his thighbone. When his leg healed, he went back to the war again. He was severely injured yet again when his troop train was blown up.

By the time Richard recovered from his third injury, the war was over, and he was now able to enter forestry school at the famous Cambridge University. Cambridge has one of the best forestry schools in the world. Studying there was quite expensive, and Richard needed a plan to earn money. One night he had a dream.

"I dreamed that I saw an aeroplane evolving into a home on wheels," he said. "It was quite clear to me how the parts could be utilized."[6] He realized that aircraft materials left from the war could be turned into caravans (the English term for vacation trailers.) They could be used to vacation in the countryside and could also be used as temporary housing for soldiers returning from the war.

The next day, Richard went to the war surplus office and bought a large number of old airplane carriages. He began to build the first recreational caravan ever made, and he later started the NAVARAC CARAVAN Company. (Can you guess how he came up with the name "NAVARAC"?)

Richard never became rich from the profit he made from his company, but he was able to make enough money selling caravans to pay his way through university.

As soon as he had completed his three-year forestry diploma in 1920, Richard applied for a job as a conservator of forests in Kenya. He was soon off on the greatest adventure of his life.

3 / Protecting Forests in Kenya

Richard Baker was lost in the forest. Again. But this time it was a vast forest of giant bamboo.

Richard had arrived in Nairobi, the capital of Kenya, in 1920. He was now thirty years old. While traveling by ship, he had had time to study Swahili, the national language of Kenya. He had studied for two hours each day with a passenger who knew the language, and when he arrived at his destination, he was able to carry on simple conversations with Kenyans. He was determined to learn even more Swahili to help him to relate well to the people with whom he would be working.

His first assignment as assistant conservator of forests was to conduct a study of a forest made up of bamboo in a region north of Nairobi. Perhaps the bamboo canes could be used as a substitute for wood to make paper?

Once he had arrived in the region, Richard led a small expedition into the forest. The average height of the bamboo canes was fifty feet, and it was very hard for the members of the expedition to make progress because the canes were very dense. Each man had to turn sideways in order to squeeze through the thick foliage. Although following the winding elephant trails was easier than moving through the bamboo, the group soon lost their sense of direction. This forest was very different than those Richard was used to in England and Canada. Even though he was using a map and compass, Richard soon became hopelessly lost.

This was Richard's first test in Africa, and already, he had endangered the lives of his men. During the day, they wandered painfully forward in a strange, greenish half-light that filtered through the dense bamboo canes. At night, their nerves were jittery as dark, shadowy figures circled around them.

The men were starting to turn against their inexperienced leader, and Richard decided to give up on his original approach and to instead use the compass to set a straight course in one direction. This meant that they had to cut through the bamboo with big knives called machetes. It was exhausting work, but the plan worked.

Similar to the first time he was lost in the forest as a child, Richard emerged in a beautiful glade. The clearing, on a mountainside, was filled with giant flowers. In

the distance, Richard glimpsed the misty peak of Mount Kenya.

From this high point, he was able to plot several clear routes through the forest on his map. Richard soon figured out the best way to navigate this type of terrain. In the course of this expedition, his team would cross this area four times, covering a thousand miles.

The greatest danger was from elephants. Richard later recalled:

It is alarming enough to come upon a mass of elephant dung, waist high, still moist and steaming and to realize that somewhere just ahead of you or even behind you were elephants. But often we would hear a deep rumbling, like distant thunder, and soon I realized that this was the rumbling from their stomachs. You may guess how I felt, knowing that the huge beasts were within twenty or thirty feet, probably scenting us and listening for our every move, standing ready to charge. . . .[7]

The bamboo samples that were gathered were found to provide excellent fiber for paper. Having survived his first assignment, Richard went on to study many forest areas in Kenya. However, he soon realized that his job as conservator was not what he thought it would be.

Kenya was a colony of the United Kingdom. A *colony* is a land that is ruled by another country. It is usually taken over by force, against the will of the local people. Like other colonies, Kenya was being exploited to enrich the British, and the local people were being treated unfairly. Instead of protecting Kenya's forests, Richard's real role was to assist the colonial powers to exploit them.

Richard began to think of ways to protect the forests so that they would not be destroyed by overuse. Local people used a method called "slash and burn" to create farms. They would cut down all the trees and bushes in a patch and burn everything. Then they could cultivate the land to grow crops. At first, the soil in the new patch would be very rich, but after a few years, the plant food or nutrients in the soil would be used up. The farmer would then move on to clear another patch.

Gradually, the old farm would become a forest again, and this cycle could go on forever. But the population of Kenya was growing larger, and there were not enough patches of land to support everyone. This was especially true now that the United Kingdom was allowing companies to come to Kenya to cut down the forests to make lumber for buildings or paper to print newspapers and books.

The forestry methods being used were not sustainable. *Sustainable* means that something can continue forever. In sustainable forestry, for example, the number of trees harvested in a year is equal to the number of new trees that replace them.

For every tree that is cut down, a new one is planted.

The unsustainable forestry methods used by the British were beginning to turn the northern parts of Kenya into a desert. The land was already dry, but with the trees gone, the wind and rain were eroding the soil. The great Sahara Desert was beginning to expand, and many people who lived in northern Kenya were forced to leave their farms behind and move south.

Richard's employer, the British Colonial Office, had not given Richard much money to plant new trees, and he had to come up with a clever but inexpensive way to restore the forests. He realized that he would have to encourage the local, Indigenous people to become conservationists and tree planters.

4 / Dance of the Trees

During his time in Kenya, Richard became very attracted to the local people. He felt especially close to the Kikuyu tribe, and he was not like most other colonial officers, who believed that white people were superior to blacks. Instead, Richard was very friendly toward Africans. He admired their cultures and religious beliefs, and he saw their way of life as superior in many ways to the way people lived in Britain.

He asked the Kikuyu elders how he could encourage the people to plant trees.

Tree planting, however, wasn't part of their culture. After hearing his proposal, the elders said, "Planting trees is God's business." Richard responded that too many trees were being destroyed and that people had to help God do this work.

The elders told him that dancing was one of the keys to everything they did. Before they planted crops, they held a dance to create enthusiasm for the work ahead. They did the same thing before the time for harvest and with other aspects of their daily life. Everything followed the rhythm of the seasons. By consulting with the Kikuyu elders, Richard had the idea of starting something new—a Dance of the Trees.

He would sponsor a big dance with prizes for the best dancers. He began to talk to the young people about his idea, and it soon became very popular. On the day of the first dance, thousands of young men and women showed up. They created a new dance to be held each year before planting trees.

Richard asked the youth to make three promises: to plant ten trees every year, to protect trees everywhere, and to do one good deed each day. He invited them to become part of a new conservation group he called the Men of the Trees. They started a tree nursery with a million new tree seedlings.

From this beginning, the Men of the Trees eventually grew to become the first international Environmental Non-Governmental Organization (ENGO). By the end of the 1930s, it would have five thousand members in over one hundred countries. All members were dedicated to the same ideal—the protection and planting of trees to heal the Earth.

Unfortunately, the colonial powers did not like Richard's approach. Instead of forcing people to do what the authorities wanted, Richard was trying to empower local people. To *empower* means to help people take action to make their lives better.

The authorities did not like this approach because of racism. *Racism* is the false belief that one race is better than others. In this case, the colonists believed the white race was superior to the black race. They thought they had the right to control and even mistreat Africans. They were afraid that empowering African people might make them revolt against white rule.

One day, Richard saw a colonial officer using a riding crop to hit the African men working for him. A riding crop is a short whip that a rider uses to hit horses to make them run faster. When the officer

tried to hit another man, Richard stepped between the officer and his victim. The blow broke Richard's collarbone. He was fired from his job for standing up for the Africans against the officer, and he was sent back to the United Kingdom.

In the United Kingdom, Richard began to travel around the country and to talk to people about his adventures in Africa. He talked about the need to plant trees and protect forests everywhere, and he started the second branch of the Men of the Trees in the United Kingdom.

Richard loved talking to children, and he even started his own radio show that had programming exclusively for children. He soon became known as "Uncle Dick."

That same year, a new government was elected in the United Kingdom, and Richard was allowed to return to colonial service, in Nigeria. This time, the area of forest he had to look after was about the size of France!

Richard thought to combine two ideas to help the Nigerians conserve forests. In

Kenya, he had learned the potential of empowering local people to achieve sustainable development by using their own cultural practices. *Sustainable development* means improving lives without damaging the environment. Richard's approach would also benefit from the new science of ecology. *Ecology* is the study of the complex relationships between living things, such as how plants and animals thrive together.

Richard began working with small farmers to create a new way of farming. He called the new type of farms *Igi Oka*, or *Tree Farms*. Instead of slashing, burning, farming, and moving on, farmers would plant perennial trees on the edges of the plots where they grew their annual crops. *Perennial* means the plant keeps growing and producing for many years. *Annual* means that the crop lasts only one season and then has to be replanted.

Trees grew very fast in this area, and the farms soon produced varieties of trees that either produced fruits and nuts or could be harvested for high-quality lumber. While the trees were growing, the annual crops could be grown among them. The young trees would help shelter the crops and prevent erosion. *Erosion* is when wind or water carries away the topsoil.

Gradually, Richard encouraged more and more farmers to use this method.

Today, this approach is called *agroforestry* or *agroecology*, and it is beginning to catch on worldwide. It is a type of farming that mimics the way trees and plants grow in nature. In a natural environment, for example, the soil is never exposed the way it is on a farm. Instead, the soil is always covered with plants. Also, in nature, one never sees a *monoculture*—that is, just one type of plant growing in an area by itself. Rather, the natural world always supports communities of different plants and animals living together. The diversity of plant and animal communities makes ecosystems more *resilient*, which means they can better withstand the forces of nature, such as erosion.

Richard traveled around Nigeria to meet with chiefs and villagers to encourage sustainable farming. To attract attention, he even brought a large gramophone with him. A *gramophone* was used at that time to play recorded music. The local people had never heard records before, and he introduced a new type of music—jazz. Then, after playing music to attract people, he would introduce his new ideas and methods for farming.

In northern Nigeria, Richard once again saw that the desert was advancing.

It was encroaching on people's farmland and forcing villagers to leave their homes, so he came up with a two-part solution to this problem. First, farmers would protect forests by carefully selecting trees for logging and then replanting them. Second, they would commit to farming in more sustainable ways, such as the tree farming Richard had encouraged.

Today, the sustainable approach to forestry and farming makes a lot of sense, now that we are aware of the problem of environmental destruction. But during Richard's time, his ideas were considered strange. Sadly, people didn't listen to Richard or put his methods into practice, and as a result, ninety percent of Nigeria's forests have been destroyed.

Even today, people are slow to adopt sustainable farming methods such as agroforestry. *Desertification*—the spreading of deserts—threatens large parts of Africa and other areas. As a result, many millions have been forced to leave their homes and become refugees in other countries.[8]

On one of his journeys in Nigeria, Richard became very ill from a tropical disease. After almost ten years in Africa, he was sent back to United Kingdom to die. On the way there, he had another near-death experience. Once again, he surprised everyone by recovering. However, the Colonial Office that oversaw his work never gave him a job again, as he was considered a troublemaker for challenging racism and environmental destruction.

5 / World Traveler

Sometimes bad experiences, such as getting fired from a job, open up new opportunities. For Richard, leaving the colonial service—working in the colonies of the United Kingdom—after ten years opened up a new world of service. He would now begin traveling to almost every country in the world to spread his core message, which was: Plant trees to save the planet!

First, Richard was invited to visit Palestine to help with tree-planting there. Most of the forests that once covered Palestine had disappeared.

In Africa, he had learned that the best way to plant trees was to rally local people. In Palestine, also known as the Holy Land, he realized that most people follow the leaders of their religion. He devised a clever plan—let's see if you think it was a bit sneaky.

The main religious groups in Palestine—Muslims, Christians, and Jews—and especially their leaders, did not like each other. They would not work together. So Richard decided to go to each leader individually and invite each one to a meeting. At the meeting, they would discuss restoring Palestine's forests. However, he did not tell them the other leaders had also been invited.

Richard asked them to arrive at different times, and as each leader arrived, Richard took him to a room that was separated by curtains from the main hall. None of the leaders could see each other, but after the last one arrived, Richard opened all the curtains. The leaders found themselves in the same room for the first time.

Quickly, Richard started the program before any of them could leave. He was very good at getting people excited about trees, and on the spot, he invited the leaders to join a Palestinian branch of the Men of the Trees. He convinced all the religious leaders to support large-scale tree planting. It helped that his idea was to ask school-children to be the main tree planters.

Interestingly, that region, which today includes the nation of Israel, is one of the only areas in the world that had more trees at the end of the twentieth century than it did at the beginning. And today, interfaith cooperation to protect the environment is a common activity in many countries. Richard's effort was one of the first of a new movement that would spread around the world.

For Richard, it was very natural to collaborate with people of all faiths. After all, he had grown up in an open-minded Christian family. Then, in Canada and Africa, he had been exposed to the religious beliefs of various Indigenous peoples. These experiences had opened up his understanding and helped him appreciate the spiritual significance of the natural environment.

In the early 1920s, Richard had attended a large conference with participants from each of the religions of the British Empire. At that conference, he gave a speech about African religions. After his talk, a woman named Claudia Skipworth Coles came up to him and said, "You are a Bahá'í." He said, "What is that?" She said,

"You respect the other person's religion as much as your own."

Claudia told Richard about the Bahá'í Faith. He was excited to learn that Bahá'u'lláh, the Founder of the Bahá'í Faith, taught that all religions were part of one great process of spiritual education. The aim of the Bahá'í Faith was to unite all humanity in one common purpose: to achieve world peace. Richard knew that religions should not be hostile toward each other and should instead work together for a better world, including a safe environment.

Soon, Richard joined the Bahá'í Faith. When he was in Palestine, he went to see the leader of the Faith, Shoghi Effendi, who was the great grandson of Bahá'u'lláh. Shoghi Effendi, who had been appointed Guardian of the Bahá'í Faith by his grandfather, 'Abdu'l-Bahá, lived at the Bahá'í World Center in Haifa. He became the first lifetime member of the Men of the Trees, and he would continue to support its conservation work for the rest of his life.

Richard often remarked that whenever he made efforts to support the Bahá'í movement, his conservation efforts thrived.

That Richard would be attracted to the Bahá'í Faith is not surprising. The Bahá'í Faith honors all the world's major religions, including the Indigenous religions to which Richard was attracted. Richard also liked that the Bahá'í writings used images of trees to explain spiritual ideas. For example, the great spiritual Educators of humanity, such as Buddha and Jesus and Bahá'u'lláh, were sometimes referred to as "the tree of life."[9] Just as trees provide delicious fruit to feed people, the tree of life feeds people's spirits with beautiful teachings.

After his travels to Palestine, Richard decided that he would go to the United States to explore its forests. He didn't have a lot of money saved up, so in order to pay for his passage, he had to work on the ship on which he was sailing. When he arrived in New York, he only had a few dollars in his pocket.

One thing that is very interesting about Richard St. Barbe Baker is that he was very lucky. There is a word for the kind of luck he experienced: *serendipity*. An example of serendipity might be finding ten dollars on the sidewalk when you don't have any money.

In New York, he had a serendipitous encounter—he ran into an old friend from the United Kingdom who invited him for a free lunch. That was the first bit of luck. While he and his friend were eating, Richard told his friend lots of exciting stories about his adventures in Africa.

Richard's second bit of luck was that the man at the next table, a well-known book publisher, overheard the stories. He went over to Richard and said, "If you can write as well as you speak, I want your book!"[10] The man stated that if Richard could write a book about Africa, he would publish it. He also agreed to pay Richard five hundred dollars, which was a lot of money at that time.

Richard wrote the book *Men of the Trees* in ten days. It would be the first of thirty books he published, mostly about—you guessed it—trees.

In New York, Richard learned that the governor of the state was a tree planter. It

was the 1930s, and the *Great Depression*—a ten-year period where millions of people did not have jobs—had just started. Richard went to meet the governor, and they discussed the idea of employing millions of men to plant trees. Later, that governor—his name was Franklin Delano Roosevelt—became President of the United States.

As President, Roosevelt started the Civilian Conservation Corps (CCC). After eight years, six million men had found jobs in the greatest conservation movement the world had ever seen. Roosevelt had created a new kind of army in a new kind of war: a peaceful army of volunteers fighting to save the Earth. Richard St. Barbe Baker is one of the people who helped shape that idea.

The success of the CCC gave Richard another, bigger, global idea, and it would emerge in the 1950s to become his major life's work. More on that later.

While in New York, Richard was also asked to give a lecture—a public talk—about Africa and tree planting. The people who published his book arranged for Richard to meet Lowell Thomas. Thomas was the popular host of *World News,* which at that time was the most popular radio show in the world, and he was fascinated by Richard's stories. He was the first person to call him the "Man of the Trees," a title by which Richard became known around the world.

At that time, public lectures were a very popular form of entertainment. After

Thomas talked about the Man of the Trees on his radio show, hundreds of people attended Richard's first lecture in the United States.

Richard had interesting experiences traveling the world, and he was a very good storyteller and became a popular lecturer. Because he was always traveling, he never had a full-time job. Lecturing became a way to help him earn enough cash to buy a ticket to his next destination.

Though Richard rarely had much money, people say that he could always acquire trees for planting! If trees were needed for a reforestation project, Richard would always be able to have them donated. Or, if he was staying in Britain, he could get them from his family's tree nursery for free.

6 / A World Vision

There are many strange and interesting stories about Richard St. Barbe Baker. Most are about trees. This story is about drums.

In the 1930s, David Hofman was one of the world's first television announcers. He worked for the British Broadcasting Corporation (BBC). The BBC operated the only public television station in the world at the time, in London. Hofman was also a friend of Richard, and in fact, they shared an apartment in London.

Hofman recalled an interview program in 1937 titled *Picture Page*, which he hosted. The program featured various VIPs (Very Important People) living in or visiting London. Hofman once invited Richard on the show to discuss his upcoming book, *Africa Drums*. Richard brought in his own drum collection, and he played African music and demonstrated how the drums were used to communicate. Richard explained that in parts of Africa, rapid communication could be achieved over long distances by interpreting drum beat patterns.

Richard had also brought along an African rain stick. He explained that African spiritual leaders used this stick to

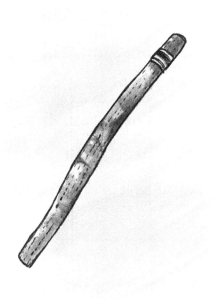

attract rain. It so happened that London
was experiencing a rare period of drought.
Hofman jokingly told Richard to use the

rain stick to make it rain, and Richard took him up on it. Before he left the radio studio, it was raining in London!

Was it just an odd coincidence? Or did the African ceremony really bring rain?

Throughout the 1930s, Richard visited forests all over the United States and Canada. Those he loved the best were California's Redwood forests, which could be found in several parts of the state. The giant redwoods were the world's largest trees, and they were endangered because logging companies wanted to cut them down to make lumber. After all, one tree was so big it could provide all the lumber for three hundred average-sized homes!

Richard joined the effort to conserve these trees, and he collaborated with the Save the Redwoods League. For eight years, he traveled back and forth between Britain and the redwoods—lecturing, building networks of support, informing the press of his work, and collecting funds—with the objective of saving the forest giants.

In 1943, Richard published another book, titled *The Redwoods*. It took several decades of effort, but eventually, over two hundred thousand hectares of the big trees were set aside in conservation areas where the trees could not be cut down.

Richard also started branches of the Men of the Trees in the United States and Canada.

Through the 1930s and early 1940s, Richard traveled the world, from Russia and Scandinavia to Australia and New Zealand. He went to India and Iran, South Africa and South America. At every location he visited, he learned about the forests and the peoples.

During his travels, Richard made hundreds of lectures and broadcasts and wrote hundreds of articles about trees. He met with mayors, with presidents, with kings, with everyday citizens, and with tens of thousands of schoolchildren. He encouraged everyone he met to plant trees to save the planet.

By the 1940s, the Men of the Trees had spread around the world, and a lot of its success had to do with Richard's magnetic personality.

Richard had a gift for inspiring people to action, and many people willingly offered to help him with his work and projects. For example, he might visit the office of a university president, a government minister, or someone else in a leadership position. Before they realized what was happening, their staff would be typing Richard's letters or book manuscript, instead of doing their regular work! People often shared their homes with him and paid for his travel. Richard's enthusiasm was infectious. Many people he met were happy to help him—and the trees—in any way they could.

It is important to say that the "Men" of the Trees was not just a group of men. Despite the name, much of its work was carried out by women. Years later, the name of the organization would change to the International Tree Foundation, reflecting the fact that both women and men were involved.

Around the time of the Second World War (1939–1945), a movement to create the United Nations began to take shape. The goal of this movement was to create a world governing body that would prevent future wars. Richard and the Men of the Trees decided to support this movement, and they moved boldly to include protecting forests in the United Nations charter. A *charter* is a formal document that states what an organization does. To meet this goal of protecting forests worldwide, invitations were sent to all of the national ambassadors in London to attend a World Forestry Charter Gathering in 1943. The gatherings were held every year until 1958, after which Richard moved to New Zealand.

Although Richard had always worked closely with individuals and communities, he also wanted the world's governments to help fulfill the Men of the Trees' goal of preserving the world's forests. The World Forestry Charter would be a document that described how governments everywhere would protect forests, and all governments would be asked to sign it once the war ended.

At the first gathering, Richard presented his analysis of the world's forestry situation. It was a gloomy picture that outlined how present forestry practices throughout the world were leading to the loss of forest cover and biodiversity and causing deserts to form. In 1947, he presented the New Earth Charter, which was a bold statement he had written about protecting the global environment. The charter was translated into many languages and shared all around the world, but it was never adopted.

Once again, Richard was ahead of his time. It was not until 1992 that the United Nations held the first Earth Summit, in Rio de Janeiro, Brazil. The Earth Summit brought world leaders together with the goal of protecting the global environment. The representatives at the summit agreed on important principles and values for a sustainable world, and they signed a non-binding Statement of Principles on Forests to guide forestry. These principles were similar to the guidelines recommended by

Richard fifty years before in his New Earth Charter.

After the Earth Summit, the representatives decided to create an Earth Charter, which was completed in 2000. Similar to Richard's earlier document, the Earth Charter is an international declaration of fundamental values and principles for building a just, sustainable, and peaceful global society in the twenty-first century. It has now been endorsed by millions of people throughout the world, just as Richard had hoped.

7 / Sahara Challenge

They had been warned. The area they were about to drive through had no roads. Instead, they would be driving on dry quicksand. No matter what, they could not stop. If they stopped moving forward, or even slowed down, their vehicle would sink into the desert, never to move again.

Richard St. Barbe Baker's team of explorers were in the middle of the Sahara Desert, hundreds of miles from the nearest settlement. It they got stuck, they would die.

It was in the middle of this dangerous stretch of quicksand that the team sighted a solitary tree in the distance. It was incredible! They had not seen a tree for four hundred miles. This lone tree would become a symbol of the reclamation of the Sahara.

Since his time in Africa, Richard had been deeply concerned about the spread of deserts, especially the Sahara Desert. The Sahara Desert was huge—it was larger than the United States and larger than the continent of Australia.

Richard believed it had once been largely forested and that the forests had been destroyed by poor farming practices dating back to the Roman Empire. Large-

scale grazing by sheep and goats introduced by the Arabs had stopped the trees
from growing back.

Richard thought the people of the
world could work together to recreate forests in the Sahara Desert. If they did, the
result would be similar to adding a new
continent to the world. Planting forests
in the Sahara would also be one way to
respond to the human population explo-
sion, which was adding billions of new
mouths to feed around the world. Richard
wrote, "To convince others, I knew that
I must have detailed information, both
with regard to the speed of the desert's
advance and to the means of stopping this

encroachment, and to the possibilities of reclamation. I decided that an ecological survey must be made and that I should lead it."[11]

To prove his theory, Richard launched an expedition. It would see him and a small team of scientists drive from the northwest side of the desert, in Morocco, to Kenya in the east. This would be a dangerous effort, as mostly there were no roads. Many desert travelers had died trying to go even part way by car.

The trip would take four months. As they left the Atlas Mountains in Algeria, in September of 1952, they saw their last

running water for two thousand miles.
Before them, for the first time, was the
great Sahara.

On their first day in the desert, Richard lost his sunglasses. They were a small part of his gear, but their loss was significant because of the glaring sun on the sand. He decided to adopt Arab headgear, which shaded his eyes and offered protection from the heat.

It was very tough going, and very tense, driving from oasis to oasis through the heart of the sun-baked desert. In some places, it was so hot that even the sand and rocks were burnt black. They were always in danger of running out of water or gasoline before reaching the next outpost.

One day, they were driving along as usual when they saw, in the distance, a large lake with African sailing boats. Lush palm trees surrounded the water. They were safe! Unfortunately, it turned out to be a mirage, an illusion created by the desert air. There was no lake. Fantastic mirages became a common sight. They ceased to wonder or attempt explanations.

Along the way, they encountered remnants of old forests. People they met told of times in living memory when there had been many trees. In the middle of the desert, they encountered a petrified forest of trees stumps. This helped prove Richard's theory that much of the desert had once been covered with forests. They had brought along a movie camera, and they filmed their discoveries.

Richard had a big dream. To reforest the desert would take a huge number of resources—money and lots of workers. Having been a captain in the army, Richard was familiar with military campaigns. He thought the desert could be "attacked" by a huge army of tree planters, using organized tactics similar to those used in warfare. Perhaps the world's armies could be used for peaceful reconstruction instead of destruction?

Richard devised a bold plan to unite all the world's governments in a single purpose. It would serve as an alternative to war, and it was a colossal vision. By uniting in a peaceful project, humanity could reclaim the world's largest desert. The Sahara, he argued, was the worst example of human environmental devastation. Reclaiming it would add millions of hectares of farm and forestland to a hungry world with a mushrooming population. The project would require a workforce equivalent to all of the standing armies of the world, some twenty million strong.

The first step was to build a Great Green Wall of trees right across the *Sahel* region. The Sahel is the dry area south of the Sahara Desert, where the desert was spreading. The wall he proposed would be twenty miles wide and 4500 miles long. It would be the largest project ever undertaken.

Richard and his team eventually made it through the Sahara. He arrived in Kenya around Christmas and met many of his old friends from his days with the first Men of the Trees. He was especially happy to be reunited with Josiah Njonjo, who was his collaborator in forming the Kenyan Men of the Trees in the 1920s. Njonjo was now head chief of the Kikuyu people.

The Sahara Reclamation Program was launched in Rabat, Morocco, in 1964. Support was received from many African heads of state. In February, Richard set out on a trip around the circumference of the Sahara and visited each of the leaders of twenty-four nations. The journey by land, sea, and air was completed on June 3. In all, Richard would travel 25,000 miles to promote his idea.

Although the leaders said they supported the plan, no one was ready to take action. Once again, Richard was far ahead of his time. It would take another fifty years before the Great Green Wall would be started.

8 / The World's Greatest Conservationist

"Someday he'll marry a tree," joked the broadcaster Lowell Thomas. He was telling his radio audience about the latest adventures of the Man of the Trees. Actually, Richard St. Barbe Baker was so busy with his trees that he didn't marry until he was fifty-six years old. Richard and his wife, Doreen Long, had two children, Angela and Paul.

He didn't marry a tree, but the Man of the Trees had to include something about trees in the wedding ceremony. As the couple left the church, they passed under an arch of spades and axes—the tools used for tree planting.

We admire heroes because they sacrifice everything for some great cause. However, the same dedication that we admire from afar may make a hero's family's life hard. Sadly, Richard's marriage did not last—probably because he was so focused on conservation and so often away from home.

In 1959, Richard married a second time, to Catriona Burnett. He was now seventy. Catriona was an independent woman who operated a large farm in the southern island of New Zealand. Richard decided to retire from his continual world travels and settle down.

One thing he planned to do was write more books. He had already published twenty books about trees, conservation, his life and experiences traveling the world, and the remarkable people he had met, especially in Africa. He even had written some bestsellers. He had also produced two novels, *Kabongo* and *Kamiti*. *Kabongo* told the story of the decline of the traditional way of life as the forests were destroyed. *Kamiti* looked into the future and showed how people came together to restore the forests. Dr. Kwame Nkrumah, the Prime Minister of Ghana, wrote the introduction to *Kamiti*. He recommended Richard's books to all who wished to understand African people.

Richard also wrote articles for *Trees*, the journal of the Men of the Trees. He had started it in 1936. Today, after eighty years, it is the oldest environmental magazine still being published.

As it turned out, Richard hated retirement. How could he rest when the world's forests were under attack? So, at the age of seventy-four, he decided to take action again. He would ride on horseback from the north of New Zealand to the south—a distance of one thousand miles—to raise awareness of the benefits of conservation. He spoke to 92,000 people on this trip—mostly schoolchildren—and encouraged them to plant and protect trees.

Catriona, who was very busy with her own work, didn't mind that her husband traveled a lot, and she even managed his travel arrangements. Throughout the 1960s and 1970s, Richard spent every summer traveling the world. He returned for a few months to New Zealand during its summer months. Sometimes his children, who still lived in Britain, would come for a visit.

Although the world's environment was continuing to deteriorate, environmental awareness was finally on the rise. People began to realize that the planet was really threatened and that Richard had been warning them about this problem for forty years. So in 1966, when Richard met with the Secretary of the Interior of the United States, Stewart Udall, to discuss conservation, Secretary Udall described Richard as "the world's greatest conservationist."[12]

Then in 1971, Richard's former school, the University of Saskatchewan, gave him an honorary doctorate in law to acknowledge his decades of environmental activism. He was now Dr. Baker!

Richard hadn't had much success alerting the world to the problem of desertification, but his luck changed by 1974.

During that year, the United Nations General Assembly passed a resolution calling for "international co-operation to combat desertification."[13]

The UN confirmed what Richard had been trying to bring to global awareness since the 1920s. Manmade deserts covered five and a half million square miles. Arid and semiarid lands, home to 628 million people, covered 36 percent of Earth's land surface. Two-thirds of all nations were being affected by the destruction of forests and other eco-systems. The total area of endangered lands was 43 percent of the world's surface.

The United Nations decided to hold the first World Conference on Desertification in 1977 in Nairobi. Richard, who was eighty-eight years old at the time, attended as the senior representative of the Bahá'í International Community. Here is what he wrote about the conference:

> 1500 delegates from 110 countries attended. I have never worked so hard in all my life keeping in touch with all these countries, many leaders of whom I had known intimately through the years and had been working with them for Desert Reclamation by tree planting. This historic conference was held at Kenyatta Centre only 18 miles

from Muguga, my old forestry station where with my old interpreter, Chief Josiah Njonjo, I had started the Men of the Trees 55 years ago. History was again made when the National Women's Council of Kenya became Men of the Trees and planned to plant 15 million trees a year for the next five years and then 30 million a year for the following five years.[14]

Richard attended a ceremonial tree planting with Chief Njonjo and Wangari Maathai, head of the National Women's Council. Maathai would later become world-famous for her tree planting efforts. Her vision of employing Kenyan women in large-scale tree planting was similar to the plan Richard had first proposed way back in 1920. Now, however, people were ready to support this idea, and millions of trees were planted. Maathai received the famous Nobel Peace Prize in 2004. Tree planting successes by Kenyan women later inspired the United Nations' Billion Tree Campaign.

Another women's conservation movement began in 1977. It was the Chipko tree-hugger movement among the Indigenous women of the Himalayan region of India, and it was started in response to the clearcutting of forests on the Himalayan slopes. Cutting down the trees was causing landslides and other problems that were threatening the mountain people's way of life.

To stop the deforestation, the women wrapped themselves around the trees to stop the loggers from cutting them down, and Richard was asked to support their campaign. Despite being eighty-eight, he visited the area twice and was very happy to hug trees with the Chipko women.

That same year, Richard visited the Soweto Township in South Africa. South Africa was in turmoil because of a racist policy called *apartheid*. The white rulers of South Africa were forcing the majority of people, who were black, to live in terrible conditions, and Soweto was a vast concentration camp, a kind of prison city. Black

South Africans were forced to live there and couldn't leave, except to work. The year before, there had been a mass protest in Soweto, and the police had opened fire on the crowds and had killed twenty-three people.

Richard believed that the local people could improve their lives by planting nut and fruit trees every time a child was born. Richard said, "A very brave woman drove me to Soweto. The highlight of my visit to this frightening all black concentration city was to a nursery school where the tiny tots sang with me: 'The more we are together the happier we'll be.'"[15] Over the

next few years, Richard succeeded in raising money to support small-scale orchard
planting in Soweto.

On July 12, 1978, Richard was invited
to Buckingham Palace in London to
receive the Order of the British Empire
(OBE)—a very high honor—from Queen
Elizabeth II. Of course, Richard managed
to slip in a few words on trees to Her Majesty, as mentioned in the letter of July 13,
written on her behalf:

Dear Dr. Baker:
The Queen has commanded me to
thank you most warmly for the kind
gift of your book yesterday [Famous

Trees of Bible Lands]. Her Majesty was particularly pleased that you were able to attend the Investiture and was also delighted to see you in such good health. She very much looks forward to reading your book.[16]

9 / Children of the Green Earth

The morning of World Environment Day—June 5, 1982—came with rain and wind. Dr. Richard St. Barbe Baker, OBE, at ninety-two years of age, was frail and sitting in a wheelchair. The people in charge of the tree-planting ceremony could not take him outside under these conditions!

Then, miraculously, just as they were about to cancel the event, the sky cleared, and the sun shone. The tree planting was on, after all!

The location was near the grave of The Right Honorable John Diefenbaker, a former prime minister of Canada, on the University of Saskatchewan campus. Richard and Diefenbaker had been among the university's first students, and they had become lifelong friends. In fact, Prime Minister Diefenbaker had helped Richard with tree-planting efforts on a number of occasions. The ceremonial tree planting would mark World Environment Day and honor Diefenbaker.

The young aspen poplar was set in the ground, and Richard somehow found the strength to get up from his wheelchair. He stood with a group of children around the tree. Together, they chanted the slogan of Children of the Green Earth: "From our hearts, with our hands, for the Earth, all the world together."[17]

After the tree was properly blessed, Richard was taken to the home where he had been staying in Saskatoon. Just as Richard entered the house, the clouds and rain returned.

Throughout his life, Richard had always thought it important to teach children about forests and tree planting. His organization, the Men of the Trees, had a children's branch called the Twigs.

When the United Nations declared 1979 the Year of the Child, Richard began to shift more attention to helping children understand the importance of protecting the environment. Educating children in ecology, he thought, was the only lasting hope that sustainability would become a core human value.

Richard began to promote the adoption of the principles of a new organization he had started, the Children of the Green Earth. He proposed that a tree be planted for every child born that year.

During his travels in the last years of his life, Richard focused on tree planning with children—including children in China. For many decades, Richard had been trying to visit China. He had wanted to ride a horse across the Gobi Desert to raise awareness about desert reclamation!

In May of 1981, Richard arrived at last in Beijing. His trip was hosted by the Chinese Academy of Forestry. Photographs from that time show him planting trees

with children, all dressed smartly in white shirts and bright red scarfs.

All did not go well, however. Richard contracted double pneumonia while on a visit to the Great Wall of China. Yet, at age ninety-one, he managed to fight it off.

In May, he made it to London for the fifty-ninth annual meeting of the Men of the Trees. Later that summer, he traveled to Nairobi, Kenya and Bombay, India, and he followed these journeys with another tour of Australia and New Zealand.

Late in 1981, Richard was back in New Zealand with Catriona. He had now reached the ripe old age of ninety-two, and his health was failing. Nevertheless, on March 27, 1982, he left New Zealand for the United States.

He spent the next two months touring for Children of the Green Earth. He participated in tree plantings and also rested while visiting the U.S. West Coast. One of the main highlights of his trip was the dedication of the Redwood National Park as a World Heritage Site, on May 22, 1982.

In early June, he flew to Saskatoon, where plans had been made to plant a tree on World Environment Day. His Saskatoon friends were shocked to see his extreme frailty.

Richard rested for several days. His flight to his next stop in Toronto was scheduled for the morning of June 9, but his friends and supporters realized he was extremely weak and were uncertain what to do.

At 8:30 a.m. that day, Richard St. Barbe Baker's earthly life came to an end in Saskatoon, where his life's work had first taken shape. He had planted his last tree and had taught his last lesson: Never give up! Never stop serving humanity! Never stop caring for the planet until the day you die!

10 / Ripple Effects

A young Australian man named Tony Rinaudo was visiting a friend's farm, and he happened to glance into a shed where a big pile of old books had been dumped on the floor. Two covers caught his attention—*Sahara Challenge* and *I Planted Trees*. Both were written by Richard St. Barbe Baker. He asked to borrow the books.

Richard's epic stories of planting trees to stop the desert inspired Rinaudo to take action. Today, he leads one of the world's most effective desert reclamation programs called Farmer Managed Natural Regeneration. It has already helped farmers in Niger restore six million hectares of farmland. That's an area larger than countries such as Costa Rica or Denmark.

When someone is a visionary, such as Richard St. Barbe Baker, his ideas are so new that people may not appreciate them. But those who "get it" may use these same ideas later on to achieve great things. Ripples from a visionary's original idea may spread out throughout the world.

You have probably thrown a pebble into a pool of water and seen the circular ripples that flow out from the central point. Though the pebble is very small,

the ripples it creates get larger and larger as they spread outward.

The term *ripple effect* is sometimes used to explain the impact that people have on others through their ideas or example. Similar to ripples in a pool, their effort is expanded by others who follow in their footsteps.

That's exactly what happened with Richard St. Barbe Baker's books and endless travels, lectures, and broadcasts. His seventy-year-long campaign of public education reached people around the world. Some of these people created little—or large—ripples of interest in protecting the planet by tree planting.

These contacts with people around the world were the most lasting and effective—though immeasurable—result of Richard's life work. St. Barbe, as his friends called him, had a unique capacity to pass his enthusiasm to others. Many foresters, for example, found their life's work as a result of hearing the Man of the Trees speak.

His efforts contributed to millions becoming aware of the importance of trees and forests to our planet. Remember the story of Felix Finkbeiner—the boy who was inspired by Richard to encourage children to plant a trillion trees? There are many others whom Richard inspired.

Take Scott Poynton, for example. In 1979, when Scott was fifteen, he chanced to hear one of Richard's radio interviews. Mesmerized by Richard's use of poetry and science to tell stories, Poynton determined to dedicate his life to protecting trees.

Scott gained a degree in forestry from Oxford University, and he went on to form The Forest Trust (TFT) in 1999. Its first goal was to ensure that all wooden furniture was made using wood from sustainably managed forests. The Forest Trust is now taking action to ensure that all products made from wood come from forests that use sustainable practices. These practices include selective felling, instead of clearcutting, and replanting trees that are harvested.

Another person influenced by Richard is wilderness champion Vance Martin. He met Richard at a famous ecovillage called Findhorn, in Scotland. He was deeply affected by Richard's love for nature and people, and he went on to become president of the Wild Foundation, chairman of the Wilderness Specialist Group of the

World Commission on Protected Areas, and international director of the World Wilderness Congress. Later, he launched Nature Needs Half, a movement to preserve half of the world in its natural state.

While Richard's vision to reclaim the world's deserts did not receive the support he had hoped in his lifetime, part of his dream is now being realized. A Great Green Wall against the Sahara is being planted by twenty-one African nations. When completed, it will be the planet's largest living structure. About fifteen percent of the wall has already been planted.

An article in *The Sunday Times* of London on July 20, 2014 acknowledged that this project was the realization of Richard St. Barbe Baker's original vision.

Richard had always had high hopes for Chinese forestry, which he saw as a model for the world. Forest cover in China had fallen to less than ten percent of land area by 1949. Richard was encouraged that it had recovered to nearly twenty percent fifty years later. In 2018, China announced plans to plant new forests that will cover another 6.6 million hectares—an area roughly the size of Ireland.

Richard always said that a third (33%) of every nation should be covered by forest. China's target is to increase forest cover from the current 21.7 percent to 26 percent by 2035, drawing closer to Richard's prescription for sustainability.

In 1949, in his book *Green Glory, Forests of the World*, Richard proposed "that all standing armies everywhere be used for the work of essential reafforestation."[18] For many years, it appeared that no nation would ever take Richard's advice. Then in 2018, China decided to give sixty thousand of its soldiers a new order: plant trees to create new forests. It was a good first step!

Through Richard's efforts, and the efforts of those with whom he collaborated or inspired, billions of trees have been protected and planted, and the work continues around the globe today. In 1992, the Men of the Trees in the United Kingdom was renamed the International Tree Foundation (ITF). ITF has helped local communities grow and protect trees in more than thirty countries. Today, it is organizing a global effort to celebrate the centenary of the Men of the Trees by planting twenty million trees in Kenya's forests.

ITF also works with children through Tree Power. Like Children of the Green Earth, Tree Power is an educational program that supports teachers and schools to inspire new generations to learn about the importance of trees.

The Men of the Trees is still active in Western Australia. Since 1979, the organization has planted over fifteen million native trees and understory plants. On July 25, 2014, with the support of two thousand people, it broke a Guinness World Record by planting over one hundred thousand trees in an hour. Recently, the organization has been renamed Trillion Trees to reflect its new focus: another challenge to the world, starting in February, 2020, to plant a trillion trees by 2050.

That, in a nutshell, is the story of the Man of the Trees. Now that you have heard it, you may want to ask yourself and your friends, what can we do to protect forests? What can we do to look after our home, Planet Earth?

Like Richard St. Barbe Baker, maybe you can move the world!

Notes

1. Greta Thunberg, "'Our house is on fire': Greta Thunberg, 16, urges leaders to act on climate," *The Guardian*, January 25, 2019. https://www.theguardian.com/environment/2019/jan/25/our-house-is-on-fire-greta-thunberg16-urges-leaders-to-act-on-climate.

2. From a letter written in 1676 by Sir Isaac Newton to Robert Hooke, quoted in "Science over time: Standing on the shoulders of giants." Science Learning Hub. https://www.sciencelearn.org.nz/resources/2612-science-over-time-standing-on-the-shoulders-of-giants.

3. For information on the Great Green Wall, please visit https://www.greatgreenwall.org/about-great-green-wall.

4. "Ethiopia plants over 350 million trees in a day, setting new world record," United Nations Environment Programme, August 2, 2019. https://www.unenvironment.org/news-and-stories/

story/ethiopia-plants-over-350-million-trees-day-setting-new-world-record.

5. Hanley, *Man of the Trees: Richard St. Barbe Baker, The First Global Environmentalist.*

6. Ibid., p. 32.

7. Ibid., p. 41.

8. Podesta, "The climate crisis, migration, and refugees," Brookings, July 25, 2019. https://www.brookings.edu/research/the-climate-crisis-migration-and-refugees/.

9. 'Abdu'l-Bahá, *Some Answered Questions,* no. 30.7.

10. Hanley, *Man of the Trees: Richard St. Barbe Baker, The First Global Environmentalist,* p. 102.

11. Ibid. p. 163.

12. Ibid. p. 220.

13. United Nations Convention to Combat Desertification, United Nations Audiovisual Library of International Law, United Nations, 2013. https://legal.un.org/avl/pdf/ha/unccd/unccd_ph_e.pdf.

14. Hanley, *Man of the Trees: Richard St. Barbe Baker, The First Global Environmentalist,* pp. 241–42.

15. Ibid., p. 244–45.

16. Ibid., p. 249.

17. Ibid., p. 261.

18. Ibid., p. 159.

Notes on Sources

This book is based on my biography *Man of the Trees: Richard St. Barbe Baker, The First Global Conservationist,* published by University of Regina Press in 2018. All quotations used in this book were taken from it. The source material for that book was found in the R. St. Barbe Baker fonds, University of Saskatchewan, University Archives and Special Collections (http://sain.scaa.sk.ca/collections/r-st-barbe-baker-fonds). The extensive collection of textual and other records, which would reach a length of 4.5 meters if lined up on shelves, includes Richard's 30+ published books and several unpublished manuscripts. Most of these books are at least semiautobiographical, and they were the main sources for his personal story and many of the quotes covering the period up to 1970. Quotes from Richard's books and other writings were used liberally to convey a sense of his voice. The innumerable clippings, diaries, notebooks, newsletters, circular letters, correspondence, and articles in the collection supplemented the material from Richard's books and provided most of the information on his life after 1970. Permission to quote liberally from Richard's books—all now out of print—and other archival material was graciously granted by his literary executors.

Bibliography

Dahl, Arthur. "The Bahá'í Approach to Trees and Forests." International Environment Forum. May 28, 2011. https://iefworld.org/ddahl99c.htm.

Hanley, Paul. *Man of the Trees: Richard St. Barbe Baker, The First Global Environmentalist.* University of Regina Press, 2018.

Podesta, John. "The climate crisis, migration, and refugees." Brookings. July 25, 2019. https://www.brookings.edu/research/the-climate-crisis-migration-and-refugees/.

Science Learning Hub. "Science over time: Standing on the shoulders of giants." New Zealand. https://www.sciencelearn.org.nz/resources/2612-science-over-time-standing-on-the-shoulders-of-giants.

Thunberg, Greta. "'Our house is on fire': Greta Thunberg, 16, urges leaders to act on climate." *The Guardian.* January 25, 2019. https://www.theguardian.com/environment/2019/jan/25/our-house-is-on-fire-greta-thunberg16-urges-leaders-to-act-on-climate.

United Nations Audiovisual Library of International Law. "United Nations Convention to Combat Desertification." 2013. https://legal.un.org/avl/pdf/ha/unccd/unccd_ph_e.pdf.

United Nations Convention to Combat Desertification. "The Great Green Wall." https://www.greatgreenwall.org/about-great-green-wall.

United Nations Environment Programme. "Ethiopia plants over 350 million trees in a day, setting new world record." August 2, 2019. https://www.unenvironment.org/news-and-stories/story/ethiopia-plants-over-350-million-trees-day-setting-new-world-record.

Suggested Reading List of Books by Richard St. Barbe Baker

Africa Drums. The Adventurers Club, 1960.
Caravan Story and Country Notebook. Self-published. 1969.
Dance of the Trees. Oldbourne Press, 1956.
Famous Trees of Bible Lands. H. H. Greaves Ltd., 1974.
Green Glory: The Forests of the World. A. A. Wyn, Inc., 1949.
I Planted Trees. Lutterworth Press, 1944.
Land of Tane: The Threat of Erosion. Lutterworth Press, 1956.
Men of the Trees. George Allen & Unwin, 1932.
My Life My Trees. Findhorn Publications, 1979.
The Redwoods. Lindsay Drummond Limited, 1943.
Sahara Challenge. Lutterworth Press, 1954.
Sahara Conquest. Lutterworth Press, 1966.